SHORT WALKS IN THE PEAK PARK

by
William and Vera Parker
with maps by P. J. Williamson

FOLLOW

Guard agains
Fasten all gat
Keep dogs un
Keep to paths
Avoid damagin **...ges and walls**
Leave no litter
Safeguard water supplies
Protect wildlife, wild plants and trees
Go carefully on country roads
Respect the life of the countryside

The route maps are based upon the Ordnance Survey map with the sanction of the Controller of H.M. Stationery Office. Printed in Great Britain.

ISBN 0 85100 0 74 6   Third Edition   © Derbyshire Countryside Ltd. 1987.

DERBYSHIRE COUNTRYSIDE LIMITED
Lodge Lane, Derby, DE1 3HE

◄ *Sheepwash Bridge at Ashford-in-the-Water*

INDEX OF WALKS

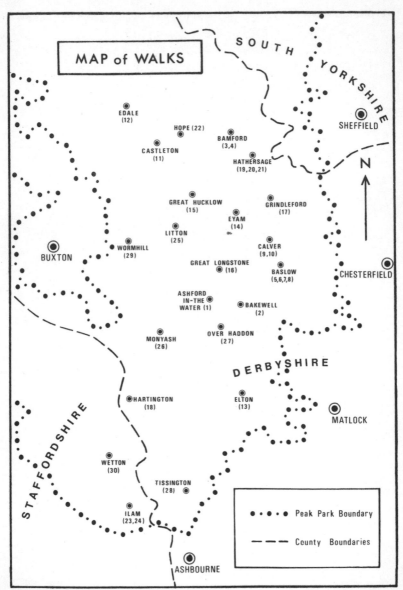

MAP of WALKS

EDALE (12)

HOPE (22)

BAMFORD (3,4)

CASTLETON (11)

HATHERSAGE (19,20,21)

GREAT HUCKLOW (15)

GRINDLEFORD (17)

EYAM (14)

LITTON (25)

CALVER (9,10)

WORMHILL (29)

BUXTON

GREAT LONGSTONE (16)

BASLOW (5,6,7,8)

CHESTERFIELD

ASHFORD IN-THE WATER (1)

BAKEWELL (2)

MONYASH (26)

OVER HADDON (27)

DERBYSHIRE

HARTINGTON (18)

ELTON (13)

MATLOCK

STAFFORDSHIRE

WETTON (30)

TISSINGTON (28)

ILAM (23,24)

SOUTH YORKSHIRE

SHEFFIELD

N

•••• Peak Park Boundary

— — County Boundaries

ASHBOURNE

4

INTRODUCTION

Our aim in writing this book of walks is to share with others the pleasure we have found on our walks in the Peak Park, and in this third edition, the very explicit instructions have been revised so that you may explore the delights of this scenic area with ease and confidence.

The Peak Park is one of the finest areas in the country for short walks. Footpaths are well-signed and maintained, and the walks over hills and moors, through peaceful valleys, along riverside paths, and on rocky crags, are delightful and varied. With the aid of this book you will be able to choose your walk, and then give all your attention to the enjoyment of your surroundings, knowing that by following the detailed instructions, you will return to your starting point without retracing your steps.

All the walks are circular, and are guided from villages in the Peak Park using only well-defined footpaths. The walks are listed alphabetically, according to the name of the village from which the walk is guided, and a map at the front of the book shows these villages, with the walk numbers.

On all the walks, information has been given on where to park your car. If you are not a motorist, you will have no difficulty in finding the starting point of a walk, since these are at well-known points in a village, or at easily-found car parks.

Although it is not necessary to use a map with this book, an Ordnance Survey one inch to the mile Tourist Map of the Peak District would add interest to your walks, and enable you to find easily the villages from which the walks commence.

This book does not give any information on the historical, botanical and geological aspects of the area, but much useful information on these subjects may be obtained from the Peak National Park Information Centres at The Old Market Hall, Bakewell, Fieldhead, Edale, and Castle Street, Castleton.

In the Peak Park many of the stiles and signposts are waymarked. A small yellow arrow sign indicates a footpath for walkers, and a blue arrow sign a bridleway.

The walks in this book are not difficult, but paths are sometimes rough and stony, and often muddy. It is advisable, therefore, to wear stout shoes or boots. The most comfortable footwear is a pair of walking boots, tried on, when purchasing, with two or three pairs of woollen socks – a guarantee against discomfort and blisters. Warm clothing and waterproofs are essential.

A particular difficulty in books of this type is that landmarks may disappear, stiles and gates can be altered or removed, and footpaths diverted. Changes in the instructions are made in new editions, but if eventually instructions do not appear to be accurate, then allowance must be made for the passage of time and the changing scene.

The Peak Park is truly a walker's paradise, and we hope that you will have the joy in following these walks that we have had in planning them for your pleasure.

William and Vera Parker

Ashford-in-the-Water – Little Longstone –
Monsal Head – Ashford-in-the-Water

STARTING POINT: *The Bull's Head*, Ashford-in-the-Water.

PARKING: Ashford-in-the-Water car park, Court Lane, between *The Bull's Head* and the church, or in the layby near the church.

WALK DESCRIPTION: Ashford-in-the-Water is a picturesque village, with its ancient Sheepwash Bridge over the River Wye near the church. You leave the village on the Wardlow road, and soon leave the road to follow footpaths to the village of Little Longstone. Walking along minor roads, you reach Monsal Head, with a magnificent view of Monsal Dale and the viaduct of the now disused railway line from Bakewell to Buxton. Continuing on the ridge high above Monsal Dale, the path soon veers away from the dale and gradually descends to a track which leads you back into Ashford.

ROUTE INSTRUCTIONS:

1. With *The Bull's Head* on your left, walk along the village street and take the first turn left, signposted 'Wardlow'.
2. 200 yards beyond the S bend, turn right on a walled path signposted 'Little Longstone 2'.
3. Pass through a stile and follow a path with a wall on your right.
4. At the end of the wall, cross a lane and go through the stile opposite.
5. Go through two stiles, and follow a path along a shallow valley.
6. Keep to the footpath, crossing three stiles, and then cross a fourth stile onto the Monsal Trail.
7. Cross the Trail, go through a stile opposite, and turn left alongside a wall.
8. Pass through a stile, keep straight on, and go through another stile.
9. Cross a stile and follow a footpath across a large field, passing an old house.
10. On reaching the road, turn left, walk through Little Longstone, and pass a small chapel on your right.
11. On reaching the T junction, cross the road and go to the right of the Monsal Head Hotel.
12. Go through the stile nearest cottages and follow the middle footpath signed 'Ashford'.

13. Cross a stile and continue along the ridge.
14. Follow the footpath, which shortly bears left, following the curve of the wall, at a sign 'Footpath'.
15. Cross a stile and continue along a track leading away from Monsal Dale.
16. Pass a dew pond and immediately turn left over a stile, following a footpath with a wall on your right.
17. At the bottom of the field, turn right over a stile, and follow a walled track.
18. On reaching the road, turn right and immediately left down Hill Cross.
19. Almost at the bottom of the hill, turn right along a track.
20. Just past the playing fields, turn left, passing behind the church.
21. On reaching the main road, turn left to *The Bull's Head*.

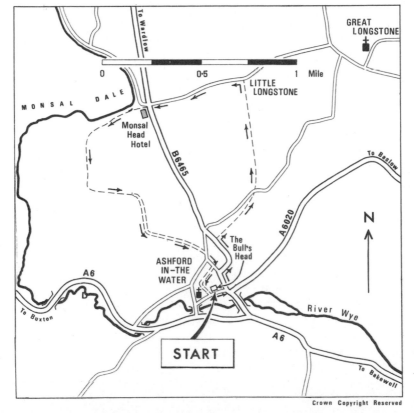

Bakewell – Coombs Farm – Bowling Green Farm – Haddon – Bakewell

STARTING POINT: *The Red Lion,* in the centre of Bakewell.

PARKING: The Market Place Car Park, Bakewell, except Mondays (market day), when a large car park is available near the Showground.

WALK DESCRIPTION: From the small market town of Bakewell, with its cattle market held every Monday, the walk takes you across the old packhorse bridge, with a delightful view of the River Wye. You continue along a level lane which passes to the rear of the Bakewell Showground, the venue of one of the largest agricultural shows in the country. The lane ascends very gradually to Coombs Farm, situated below the extensive Manners Wood, and continues along a peaceful valley. Tracks lead you past Bowling Green Farm and over Haddon Tunnel to the River Wye, where you follow a riverside path for a short distance. Field paths then lead away from the river to the drive through the Showground, where you cross the river to return to the Market Place in Bakewell.

ROUTE INSTRUCTIONS:

1. With *The Red Lion* on your right, walk along the main road and cross the river bridge.
2. Bear right to Station Road, and in 50 yards turn right to Coombs Road.
3. Keep straight on for ¾ mile and pass under a railway bridge.
4. Keep straight on for ¼ mile and pass Coombs Farm.
5. From Coombs Farm, keep straight on the track and in ½ mile follow the bend of the track to the right.
6. 200 yards from the bend, at a fork of tracks, bear right.
7. Keep straight on for ¼ mile, and leave the track where it turns left to Bowling Green Farm, to keep straight on at the signpost 'Bridleway'.
8. Keep straight on, along a wooded path.
9. Pass through a waymarked gate and follow a path with railings on left.
10. Go through two gates and then bear left alongside the railings.
11. Go through a gate and turn left along a track, passing over the tunnel of a disused railway where the track bends to the right.
12. In 500 yards turn right through a swing gate at the signpost 'Public Bridleway to Coombs Road', and in 100 yards bear left at the signpost 'Public Bridleway'.

13. In 200 yards bear left to the riverside path at the signpost 'Public footpath to Bakewell'.

14. Cross a small plank bridge, and keep straight on, with a hedge on your right all the way to the Showground.

15. On reaching Bakewell Showground, walk to the far end, and turn left over a concrete bridge.

16. In 100 yards, cross the river bridge and turn right on the riverside path.

17. In 70 yards turn left through an opening in the wall to the market place, and turn left at the main road to *The Red Lion*.

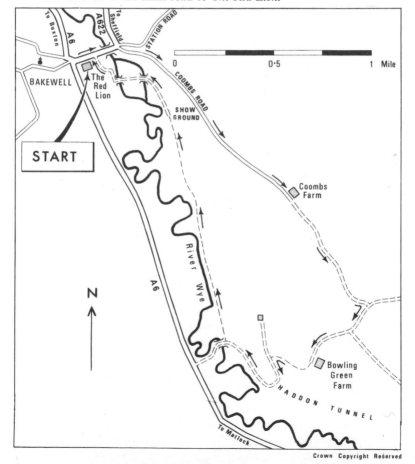

9

Ladybower Reservoir — Thornhill — Win Hill —
Yorkshire Bridge — Ladybower Reservoir

STARTING POINT: The *Yorkshire Bridge Inn*, Ladybower Reservoir.
Directions: From Bamford, with the church on your right, take the A6013 Sheffield road for 1 mile, and the *Yorkshire Bridge Inn* is on your left.

PARKING: By the side of the reservoir, just past the *Yorkshire Bridge Inn*.

WALK DESCRIPTION: After parking your car by the beautiful Ladybower Reservoir, return to the *Yorkshire Bridge Inn* to start your walk. A quiet road leads you across the Yorkshire Bridge and alongside the River Derwent, before it ascends to the small hamlet of Thornhill. Turning right in Thornhill, you gradually climb the slopes of Win Hill on a path with superb views of the Derwent Valley and Bamford Edge. Just before reaching a fir wood, you see the Ladybower Reservoir and the woods surrounding it. A steep and very rocky path descending through the fir wood returns you to the Yorkshire Bridge and the road back to your starting point.

ROUTE INSTRUCTIONS:

1. With the *Yorkshire Bridge Inn* on your right, walk along the main road, and in 200 yards turn right at the signpost 'Thornhill 1½ miles'.
2. Keep to this road, which bends left at the Yorkshire Bridge.
3. On reaching Thornhill turn right at the signposted road junction.
4. After passing a chapel on your left, turn right at the 'No through road' sign.
5. Follow the lane, which leads to a footpath, and keep straight on up the hill.
6. Pass through a stile and a gate, still ascending hill.
7. At next gate keep right, up steep bank, to join sunken track.
8. On reaching a fir wood, turn right in a few yards over a stile, and go downhill, through the woods, ignoring all side paths.
9. On reaching the broad track by the river, turn right.
10. Take the first turn left over the bridge, and continue up the road to the main road, where you turn left to the *Yorkshire Bridge Inn*.

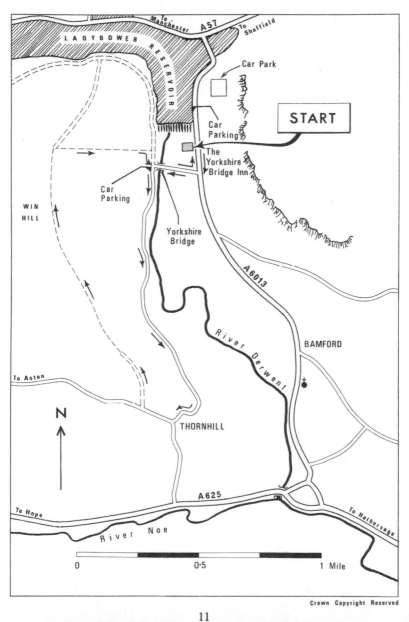

Bamford Station – Thorp –
Hurst Clough – Bamford Station

STARTING POINT: Bamford Station approach road.

PARKING: Bamford Station approach road.
Directions: From Bamford, with the church on your left, follow the main road for ¾ mile, and just past a service station, turn left into Saltergate Lane, immediately crossing the bottom of the lane into the station approach road.

WALK DESCRIPTION: This is a delightful walk, in quiet countryside, first leading you around the peaceful Sickleholme golf course, where every effort should be made not to disturb the golfers in their game, and where you should keep a sharp look-out for flying golf balls. On this part of the walk you have a good view of the Hope valley, with the Mam Tor to Lose Hill ridge in the background. After leaving the golf course, you pass through the tiny hamlet of Thorp, which consists only of a farm and a few cottages. On the minor road, just beyond Thorp, another view opens up – of Stanage Edge, Higger Tor, and Millstone Edge. From this minor road, field paths take you past another farm at Hurst Clough, and from there you return, by a steeply-descending lane, to the residential area along Saltergate Lane and back to your starting point.

ROUTE INSTRUCTIONS:

1. Turn right out of the Station approach road, along Saltergate Lane, passing Sickleholme Golf course, and at the top of the lane, just before a T junction, turn right over a stile, at the signpost 'Thorp 1'.

2. Keep straight on, along the top side of the golf course, and turn right by a fence at far side of course.

3. In 100 yards, turn left at the fence corner.

4. In 50 yards, at the 13th hole, turn left, and cross an iron bridge.

5. Bear left along a wide track, follow a right-hand bend, and enter the golf course again.

6. Turn immediately left, passing the 13th tee, and walking behind the 12th hole, to follow the path alongside the hedge.

7. Where the hedge bends left, bear right to a barn and turn left.

8. Cross a stile by a gate, signed 'Footpath' and keep straight on in the direction of a distant farm.

9. Cross two stiles and a stream, and immediately turn left over a stile.

10. Ascend the field to a gap in the hedge.

11. Keep straight on up the next field and go through a gap in the hedge.

12. Keep straight on to a fence stile. Keep to the left of farm buildings and cross a stile at the far end.

13. Turn left up a lane near the farmhouse, and turn left at the T junction.

14. In 90 yards, bear left at the Y-junction.

15. In 100 yards, turn left through a swing gate, at the signpost 'Public Bridleroad to Hurst Clough and Bamford', and immediately bear right along a path, with a row of trees on your right.

16. Pass through a swing gate, and turn sharp left, with a fence on your left.

17. At the bottom of the field, go through a gate and cross a stream.

18. Walk alongside a fence and go over a stile.

19. Follow a track signed 'Bridleway' and at a junction of tracks turn left.

20. Follow the track to the top of Saltergate Lane, where you turn left back to your starting point.

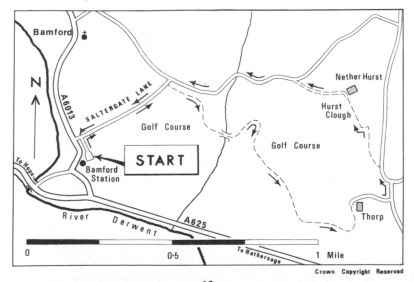

13

Baslow – Bubnell – Calver – Curbar – Baslow Edge – Baslow

STARTING POINT: Baslow Car Park.

PARKING: Baslow Car Park, adjacent to *The Cavendish Hotel*, on the Nether End (east) side of Baslow.

WALK DESCRIPTION: From the Nether End district of Baslow, the route first follows the main road to Baslow Church, with its unusual clock face, commemorating the Jubilee of Queen Victoria in 1897. After crossing the ancient stone bridge, with its tiny toll-house, you follow a lane along the riverside to the hamlet of Bubnell, passing the seventeenth-century Bubnell Hall. Field paths and riverside paths then lead to Calver. From Calver there is a long climb up steep roads through the village of Curbar to the top of the ridge at Curbar Gap. Your efforts will be rewarded as you walk along Baslow Edge, with a panoramic view over miles of rolling countryside. On reaching the Wellington Monument you will have a magnificent view of the Derwent Valley. An easy walk downhill leads to a residential area on the outskirts of Baslow, and to your starting point.

ROUTE INSTRUCTIONS:

1. Turn left out of the car park, and with *The Cavendish Hotel* on your left, walk along the main road and bear right at the junction.
2. Just past Baslow church turn left over the bridge, and then turn right.
3. After ½ mile, just before the lane bends to the left, turn right through a stile and cross the field diagonally left to another stile.
4. Follow the path under the telephone wires for 100 yards, and then keep straight on, keeping by the wall.
5. Cross a stile and follow the path through a wood.
6. At the end of the wood, pass through a stile, and follow footpath by the river.
7. Cross two stiles and go over a bridge, following the track by the river.
8. Pass under a concrete bridge, and turn right over the old bridge at Calver.
9. At the end of the bridge, turn left, and walk up the hill signposted 'Curbar village'.
10. At the crossroads, keep straight on at the signpost 'Curbar Edge'.
11. When the road bends left, keep straight on through a stile and up the fields, to meet the road again at Curbar Gap.

12. Turn right along the road, and in 150 yards, turn sharp right to cross a stile, bearing right from the wide track in 30 yards to follow an indistinct path to Baslow Edge.

13. Follow the path along the edge until you are within 100 yards of the Wellington Monument, and then turn right down the broad track.

14. Follow this track downhill until you reach a surfaced road on the outskirts of Baslow.

15. Take the second road on the left (Eaton Hill), and on reaching the main road in Baslow, cross the main road and the village green back to the car park.

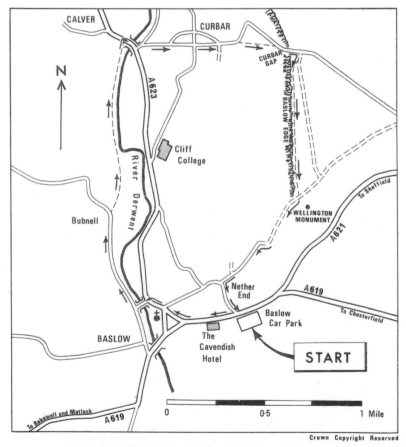

Baslow – Curbar – Over End – Baslow

STARTING POINT: Baslow Car Park

PARKING: Baslow Car Park, adjacent to *The Cavendish Hotel*, on the Nether End (east) side of Baslow.

WALK DESCRIPTION: This is a level, pleasant walk, which first passes through a residential area of Baslow, and continues through fields and along footpaths, with impressive views on your left of the Derwent valley and Longstone Edge. After passing through a farmyard, you continue along a lane, which, in wet weather, is extremely muddy. Here, the gritstone ridge of Baslow Edge rises high on your right. Following field paths and tracks, you arrive at the village of Curbar, and then descend, by a quiet lane, passing by Cliff College, a Methodist Training College, to the main road. After a short distance on the main road, you steadily climb a country lane, to return, through a residential area, to Baslow.

ROUTE INSTRUCTIONS:

1. From Baslow car park, go straight across the village green and up the road opposite (Eaton Hill).

2. At the top of the hill, turn right on Bar Road.

3. In 100 yards turn left along Gorse Bank Lane, and at the end of the houses continue along a narrow lane.

4. At the end of the lane, keep straight on through the farmyard, and along a lane which is partly paved.

5. At the end of the lane, go through a stile and bear left to a stile.

6. Follow the path through two rock-strewn fields, signposted 'Curbar'.

7. Immediately after passing houses, turn left through a gate signposted 'Curbar', and walk diagonally down the field to a stile in the bottom corner.

8. Near the end of the wall on your left, bear right to a wooden stile, to follow a path with a wall on your right.

9. Go through a stile and along a walled path.

10. At the house on your right, keep straight on.

11. Pass through a stile onto a walled track.

12. On reaching the road, turn left into Curbar village.

13. At the crossroads, turn left at the signpost 'Cliff College' and follow the lane till you reach the main Calver to Baslow road.
14. Turn left along the main road for ¼ mile, and then bear left up the lane signed 'Unsuitable for heavy goods vehicles'.
15. Continue along this lane, which eventually leads into Over Road.
16. At the T junction, turn left.
17. Take the first turn right down Eaton Hill back to your starting point.

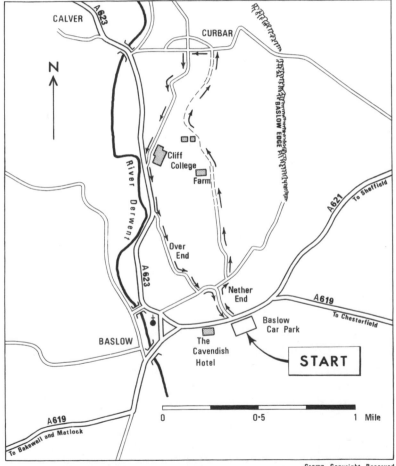

Chatsworth Park – Calton Lees – Edensor – Chatsworth Park

STARTING POINT: Calton Lees Car Park, Chatsworth Park, near the southern entrance.

PARKING: Calton Lees Car Park, Chatsworth Park.
Directions: To reach the Car Park from Baslow, take the A619 Bakewell road, and in ½ mile keep straight on the B6012 Matlock road to Chatsworth Park. Drive through the park to the far end, keeping on the main road. The car park is on your right, just after crossing a cattle grid.

WALK DESCRIPTION: On this walk you pass through the pretty hamlet of Calton Lees, with its attractive houses and gardens. A track then brings you to Calton Houses, and after a sharp right hand bend you soon see Russian Cottage on your right. After passing through New Piece Wood, you follow a footpath through parkland to Edensor – a model village built to house estate employees. The walk continues along a path over a low hill, with fine views of Chatsworth House and the cascade waterfall. On reaching the graceful bridge spanning the River Derwent, you return to the car park along a peaceful riverside path. Chatsworth House is open between Easter and October.

ROUTE INSTRUCTIONS:

1. From the car park continue along the car park drive, away from the main road, and go through a wooden gate by the sign 'No Through Road'.

2. On reaching a grass triangle at a T-junction in the hamlet of Calton Lees, walk straight forward, and through the middle gate of three, marked 'All dogs on leads'.

3. Follow the track, which, after one mile, winds right and left, passing a farm and Calton Houses.

4. 100 yards beyond the last cottage, go through a wooden gate and turn right.

5. Follow the track, which passes to the left of a barn, signposted 'Public footpath to Edensor and Chatsworth'.

6. Cross a stile and follow the track through woods to a ladder stile.

7. Keep straight on, downhill, passing along the left edge of two tree enclosures, and walking in the direction of Edensor church spire.

8. On reaching the fence surrounding Edensor churchyard, turn left, with the churchyard on your right, and go through an iron swing gate at the top of five steps.

9. Go down a long flight of steps to Edensor village.

10. Turn right on the road and walk straight on through the village to the main gates.

11. Cross the road and take the path opposite, which bears diagonally right.

12. On reaching the bridge, turn right along the riverside path, with the river on your left.

13. On reaching a ruined mill, turn right up the hillside back to the car park.

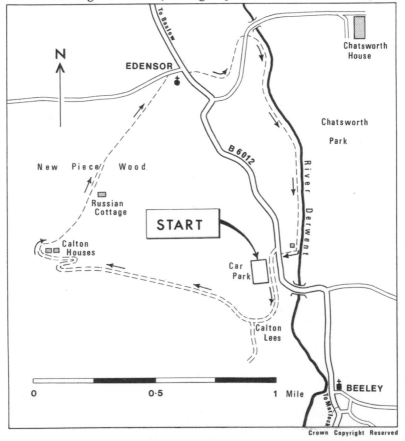

BASLOW – WALK 8 4 MILES

Chatsworth Park – Chatsworth House –
Hunting Tower – Waterfalls – Chatsworth Park

STARTING POINT AND PARKING: See Walk 7.

WALK DESCRIPTION: Anyone visiting the Peak Park will wish to explore Chatsworth Park, and this walk will take you to the House and garden, the Hunting Tower, the waterfalls, and through the park. The start of the walk is on a riverside path by the peaceful River Derwent. After one mile you cross the picturesque Chatsworth bridge and walk towards Chatsworth House. Passing on the left of the House, the walk goes by Chatsworth Farmyard, which is open to the public, and then turns left through a wood, and up a long flight of steps to the Hunting Tower. To avoid the steep steps, keep on the main drive at point 6, and go left around a hairpin bend to the tower. A waymarked path leads to the top of the waterfalls, and from that point one has an extensive view of the garden and parkland. The walk then continues through the estate and along a moorland path, to return, by a rural lane to the car park. Chatsworth House and Farmyard are open between Easter and October.

ROUTE INSTRUCTIONS:

1. From Calton Lees Car Park walk to the cattle grid nearby on the main road through the park, and follow the path down the field to the river.
2. Follow the riverside path to the left for one mile.
3. On reaching Chatsworth bridge, turn right and then immediately right along the path towards Chatsworth House.
4. Walk up the drive to the clock tower, and follow the path to the left round the tower to the drive.
5. Bear right on the drive to a gate near the 'Farmyard' sign.
6. Keep to the main drive, and 100 yards beyond a right bend, turn left on a woodland track just before a waymark stone, and opposite a barn. (To avoid steps at point 7 see 'Walk Description').
7. Keep straight on at a crossing of tracks, cross a stream, and ascend 144 steps to the Hunting Tower.
8. Go to the right of the Hunting Tower and follow a waymarked narrow footpath on the right, opposite to a sunken door of the tower.
9. Follow the blue arrow waymarks through the woods, ignoring side paths, and climb a short flight of steps to the top of the Cascade waterfalls.
10. With your back to the waterfalls, climb six steps to the main track and turn right.

11. Keep straight on this track for ½ mile, and on joining a surfaced drive, turn left. At a crossroad of tracks, turn right at the yellow arrow waymark sign.

12. Cross a stile by a gate and follow a wide moorland track turning right in 150 yards at a waymark sign on a post, and crossing the moor diagonally left.

13. Go over a stile by a wooden gate and cross a field towards a farm, cross a stile and turn right down a lane.

14. Keep straight on down the lane, and turn right at the main road. Cross the bridge into Park, and take the path on left back to car park.

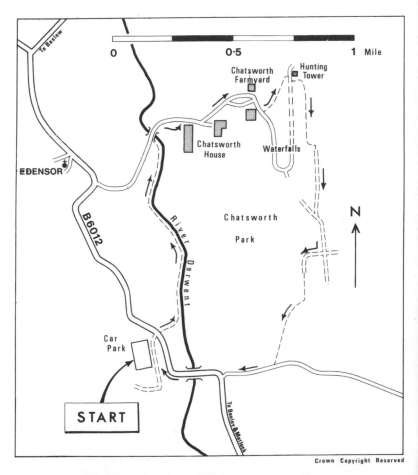

CALVER – WALK 9   5 MILES

Haywood Car Park – Froggatt Edge – Curbar Edge – Curbar – Froggatt – Grindleford – Haywood Car Park

STARTING POINT: Haywood Car Park – 2½ miles from Calver.

PARKING: Haywood Car Park.
Directions: To reach the car park from Calver crossroads, take the B6001 Hathersage road, and in 300 yards, turn right onto the B6054 Sheffield via Froggatt Edge road. The car park is on your left in 2½ miles, 300 yards past a left hand bend.

WALK DESCRIPTION: On this walk you will enjoy superb views of the Derwent Valley and Middleton Dale, as you walk along the level track on the high escarpments of Froggatt Edge and Curbar Edge. These are extremely popular ridges for climbers, especially at weekends, and you will be able to pause and admire their skill on these high crags. From Curbar Edge you descend to Curbar, and after an interesting walk along its quiet lanes, cross the main road to Froggatt, with its old stone bridge over the River Derwent. You soon enter Froggatt Wood, which is National Trust property, and on reaching Grindleford Bridge on the main road, climb quite steeply, through woodland, back to the car park.

ROUTE INSTRUCTIONS:

1. At the far end of the Haywood Car Park, go over a stile and cross a stream to reach the main road in 100 yards.
2. Turn right on the road, and in 50 yards bear left through a swing gate at the Peak National Park sign.
3. Keep on along Froggatt Edge on the broad path for about one mile.
4. Ascend a rocky slope to Curbar Edge.
5. After about one mile, the track gradually descends, and passes through a swing gate to the road.
6. Turn right down the road, and in 200 yards turn left through a stile by a 'Curbar Gap' and 'Footpath' sign.
7. Keep on the path through six fields and re-join road at lower level.
8. Continue down the road for 300 yards and then turn right, opposite a footpath sign, along a lane between cottages, which passes through a residential area.
9. At the well and the round stone trough, turn right.

10. Keep straight on along this road for ¾ mile until you reach the crossroads.

11. Cross the main Sheffield to Calver road and go down the lane opposite at the signpost 'Froggatt'.

12. At Froggatt Bridge keep straight on through the village and walk along a high railed pavement.

13. At the end of the pavement keep straight on the 'No Through Road' at the signpost 'Public footpath to Grindleford Bridge.'

14. The lane leads into a walled track.

15. Go through a stile and bear right at the wall corner to a stile.

16. Follow the path, with a wall on your left.

17. Cross two fields and stiles, and enter Froggatt Wood at the N.T. sign.

18. Cross a stone bridge over a stream, and keep on the main stone-paved path through the woods.

19. Pass through a stile into an open field, and keep straight on.

20. In the next field turn left through a wicket gate, and bear diagonally right to a wicket gate opening onto the main road through Grindleford.

21. Turn right along the road, and in 30 yards, just before reaching the church, turn right along a walled track.

22. Where the track bends right, turn left over a stile into a wood.

23. Walk straight on, uphill, through the woods, keeping to the main path.

24. The path eventually bears right by a stone wall, and leads onto a track.

25. Bear right on the track and keep straight on, passing over a stile, to car park.

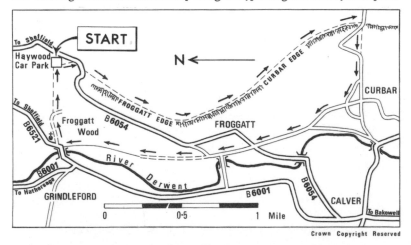

Calver – Froggatt – Curbar – Calver

STARTING POINT: *The Derwentwater Arms,* Calver.

PARKING: Near *The Derwentwater Arms,* Calver.
Directions: From the main Calver crossroads, take the residential road, situated between the Bakewell and Baslow roads – Sough Lane. *The Derwentwater Arms* is on the right.

WALK DESCRIPTION: This is an easy, level walk, mainly along riverside paths by the River Derwent. You walk through Calver to the main road, with its ancient and new bridges side by side, and then continue along field and riverside paths to the pretty village of Froggatt, which lies in the shelter of the high crags of Froggatt Edge. After crossing the ancient packhorse bridge, you continue your walk along a lane, almost to the village of Curbar, where you return, by a field path, to the river. An interesting walk by the river will lead you back to Calver.

ROUTE INSTRUCTIONS:

1. Facing *The Derwentwater Arms,* take the lane on the left of the inn.
2. At a junction of roads, turn left along Main Street, and keep straight on until you reach the main Calver to Baslow road.
3. Cross the road and turn right, bearing left from main road in 30 yards.
4. Just before reaching the bridge, turn left along a surfaced track opposite a signpost 'Public footpath' (Calver Mill).
5. Keep straight on, keeping left of stream.
6. Follow the track, with a barn on your left, and go over a stile.
7. Follow the path across a field, turning left at the end of the field to follow a riverside path.
8. Pass through a stile and continue along the path, with the river on your right, until you reach the main road.
9. Cross the road and go through the stile opposite.
10. Follow the path to a concrete bridge.
11. Cross the bridge and follow riverside path, with river on your right.
12. On reaching Froggatt Bridge, cross a stile and turn right over the bridge.
13. At the end of the bridge, turn right along the road, and keep straight on to the crossroads.
14. At the crossroads, keep straight on following 'Curbar' signpost.

15. In ¼ mile, just past Ridding House Farm, and opposite Glen Cottage, turn right through a stile.

16. Walk diagonally right across a field and go through a stile.

17. Follow the path diagonally right to the weir, and then turn left along the riverside path, with the river on your right.

18. Cross a plank bridge and a wooden stile.

19. Cross a wooden stile onto a minor road and turn right.

20. Continue along the road until you reach *The Bridge* inn at a junction of roads, and then turn right, crossing an iron-railed footbridge.

21. At the end of the bridge, immediately turn left along a track.

22. Pass under bridge, and immediately turn right up a flight of steps.

23. Keep straight on the main road for 150 yards, and turn left at the signpost 'Calver Village'.

24. Keep straight on to the centre of Calver, and bear right at the fork of roads back to *The Derwentwater Arms*.

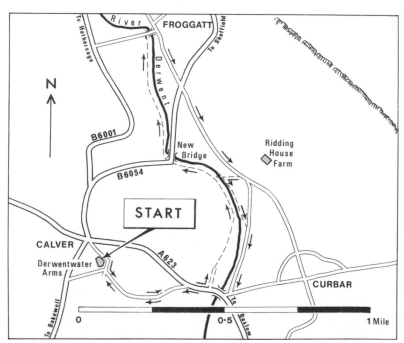

Castleton — Hollins Cross — Mam Tor — The Winnats — Castleton

STARTING POINT: Castleton Car Park.

PARKING: Castleton Car Park, on the main road, near *The Bull's Head*.

WALK DESCRIPTION: Choose a clear day for this walk, as there are spectacular views of the Hope and Edale valleys from the ridge between Hollins Cross and Mam Tor. This well-known and popular walk starts in Castleton and follows a lane to the foot of the hills. From here you climb very steeply up a well-maintained and stepped path to the viewfinder at Hollins Cross. After this fairly strenuous climb, the rest of the walk is easy, and you will enjoy a scenic walk along the ridge from Hollins Cross to Mam Tor. From the summit of Mam Tor you descend, by a stepped path, to the road at Mam Nick, and then follow field paths to Winnats Pass. Descending steadily through the pass, with its magnificent high crags on either side, you pass Speedwell Cavern, and the near-by gift shop, which sells articles made of the locally-mined 'Blue John' stone. You return, by field paths, to the old part of Castleton, passing by Peveril Castle and the entrance to Peak Cavern. Your return to the car park is alongside a picturesque stream.

ROUTE INSTRUCTIONS:

1. Follow a footpath beside a stream, on the car park boundary, which leads away from the main road.
2. Turn left at lane, and keep straight on.
3. At the second left bend in the lane, go over a stile signed 'Public footpath to Back Tor' and follow a steep path up the hillside.
4. At the Hollins Cross viewfinder, turn left along the ridge (Bridleway to Rushup Edge).
5. After passing the summit of Mam Tor, descend a flight of steps to the road at Mam Nick, and immediately turn left along a path which descends a field.
6. Cross a road by two stiles.
7. At a junction of paths, bear to your left, keeping to the left of a small quarry.
8. Cross a road by two stiles.
9. Cross five stiles, and then turn left down a road into Winnats Pass.

10. Turn right over a stile, 25 yards past the Speedwell Cavern.
11. Go through a stile and then follow a path bearing left by a wall.
12. Continue along this path, which leads into a lane, where you will see Peak Cavern and Peveril Castle on your right.
13. Cross a stream, and immediately turn left along a track beside the stream to the car park.

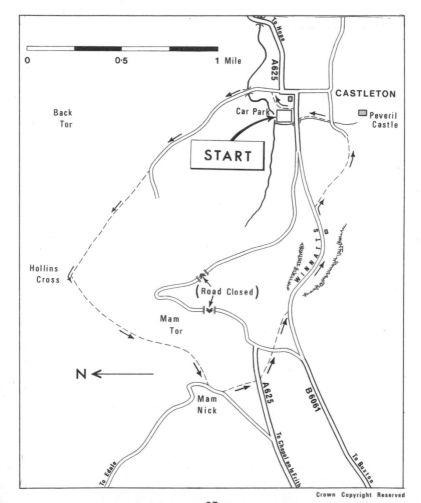

27

Edale – Upper Booth – Barber Booth – Edale

STARTING POINT: Edale Car Park.

PARKING: Edale Car Park.
The car park is situated ¼ mile south of Edale, near Edale Station.
Directions: Turn right off the road from Hope, just before a right turn into Edale.

WALK DESCRIPTION: Edale is an attractive if rather isolated village near the end of the Vale of Edale. It is very popular with walkers, since it is the starting point of the Pennine Way, and for walks across Kinder Scout. This is an easy, level walk, with excellent views of the valley and the surrounding hills. You walk into the village from the car park, and then follow a footpath running along the lower slopes of Broadleebank Tor. As you follow this footpath, pause for a moment to admire the sweep of the Edale valley and the range of hills on your left. On the left of the ridge is Lose Hill, leading to Back Tor, Hollins Cross, Mam Tor and Rushup Edge. The path descends to Upper Booth, and then turns towards Barber Booth, returning through fields to the car park.

ROUTE INSTRUCTIONS:

1. From Edale car park leave by the exit near the toilets and turn right along the road to Edale village.
2. On reaching the *Old Nag's Head*, Edale, turn left at the signpost 'Public footpath to Upper Booth 1½'.
3. Go through a swing gate and follow a footpath signed 'Pennine Way'.
4. At the top of the tree-lined path turn left over a stile at the signpost 'Public footpath to Hayfield via Upper Booth and Jacob's Ladder'.
5. Cross a field diagonally right to a stile.
6. Cross three fields to a 3-stepped stile.
7. Cross a very high stile and continue along path beside row of trees.
8. Cross a three-stepped stile, and in 100 yards keep straight on, ignoring the sign 'To open country'.
9. Pass through a stile and walk down the hill through hillocks to a stile.
10. Continue down the hill, passing through two stiles.
11. Go over a stile by a gate, along path, which leads into walled lane.

12. At the T junction of tracks, turn left for 20 yards and go through the first gate on your left signed 'Public footpath to Barber Booth'.

13. Cross a stile, a small bridge, and another stile, and then follow the path through a field, with a fence on your right.

14. Cross a stile and turn right along the path to another stile.

15. Cross a field diagonally left to a stile, and follow a farm track.

16. At a gateway keep straight on, with the railway lines immediately on your right.

17. The track bends right over a railway bridge, and then left, passing through a farmyard.

18. Pass in front of a row of cottages and keep left, passing Edale Methodist Chapel on your left.

19. At the T junction turn left along the lane, and in 100 yards bear left through a wicket gate at the signpost 'Edale'.

20. Pass over a railway bridge and turn right through a wicket gate.

21. Cross 'Edale' waymarked stile and follow footpath through three fields.

22. Cross a field slightly left, in the direction of a marked tree, and cross a stile and bridge over a stream.

23. Go across the farm drive and cross another stile.

24. Follow the footpath sign on a tree to the next stile beside a brook.

25. Keep straight on to the road, and turn right to the car park.

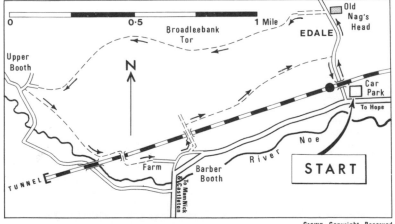

Crown Copyright Reserved

Elton – Robin Hood's Stride –
Birchover – Elton

STARTING POINT: Elton Church

PARKING: In Elton.
No official car park.
Directions to Elton from Bakewell – From Bakewell, take the A6 Matlock road for 2 miles, turn right on the B5056 Ashbourne road, and in 1¼ miles, turn left. In 2¾ miles turn right at the signpost Elton.

WALK DESCRIPTION: A visit to the curiously-shaped rocks, known as Robin Hood's Stride, and to the pretty village of Birchover, is made on this interesting walk. Following field paths from Elton church, you reach a quiet lane, which will lead you to Robin Hood's Stride – so named, since the distance between the pinnacles of rock was believed to measure the length of his stride. From this viewpoint you descend by a track to the main road, and then climb a steep path, where, on looking back, you have a fine view of the rocks, which from this point resemble a fortress on a hill. Soon you reach Birchover, where you may wish to visit a museum of Bronze-age relics, and Rowtor Rocks, behind *The Druid Inn,* where steps and armchairs were carved in the rocks by a local parson in the 18th century, so that he could enjoy the view. Continuing through the village, you pass through Upper Town, with its well-preserved stocks, and complete your walk along narrow lanes and back to Elton.

ROUTE INSTRUCTIONS:

1. From Elton church, go down Well Street, and in 40 yards, bear left along a track, at the signpost 'Public footpath to Youlgreave.'

2. In 50 yards, where the track bends right, go through a gate and turn left for 20 yards.

3. Turn right by a free-standing stile, and follow a footpath down the field, keeping to the hedge on your right.

4. Cross a stile and keep straight on across a field to another stile.

5. Cross a corner of a field, diagonally right to a stile, and then walk diagonally left, up the hillside, through three more fields, to the road.

6. Turn right along the road, and keep straight on for ¾ mile.

7. Look out for the strangely-shaped Robin Hood's Stride rocks on your right, and 300 yards on, turn right, through a stile, at footpath signpost.

8. Bear right towards the rocks, crossing two fields.

9. On entering the rocks area, turn left along a track, following a wall on left.

10. Keep straight on down the track, and turn right at a farm road.
11. Turn left for a few yards along a lane, and left again onto the main road.
12. In 150 yards, turn right over a stile, at the signpost to Birchover.
13. Keep straight on up the hillside, and bear left, and then right, keeping around the base of a copse of trees on a hill.
14. Pass through a stile, and on reaching a U-bend track, take the lower track.
15. Pass through gates into a walled lane, and follow the lane until you reach *The Druid Inn*, in Birchover.
16. Keep straight on up the main village street, and turn right, opposite the Post Office, on the road marked 'Unsuitable for Motors'.
17. Keep straight on for ¼ mile to Upper Town, and straight on again along the single track road.
18. Follow this lane for ¾ mile, and on reaching the T junction, turn right.
19. In 100 yards, at the crossroads, keep straight on, at the signpost Elton, for one mile, to Elton church.

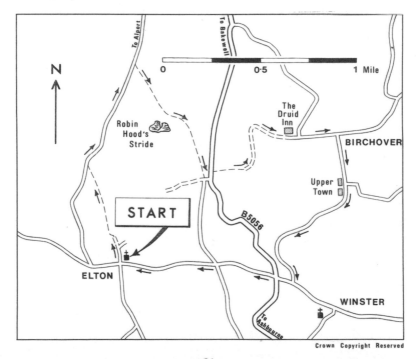

Eyam – Foolow – Bretton – Eyam

STARTING POINT: Eyam Car Park.

PARKING: Eyam Car Park.
Directions: Drive along the main street of Eyam, with the church on your right, and just past *Ye Old Rose and Crown* turn right up Hawkhill Road. The car park is immediately on your right.

WALK DESCRIPTION: This walk commences at Eyam – a village renowned for the self-sacrifice of the people of the village, who, in 1665, voluntarily isolated themselves, to prevent the spread of infection when the Great Plague of London was carried there in a box of clothing. Your walk from Eyam follows well-signed footpaths to the typically-Derbyshire village of Foolow, and then steadily climbs a minor road to *The Barrel Inn* at Bretton – a 1,300 feet high inn, with old oak barrel seats and panoramic views. The walk follows a footpath down the hillside, passes through a fluorspar works, and returns to Eyam along the main road.

ROUTE INSTRUCTIONS:

1. Turn left out of the car park, and right along the main road.
2. Take the first road on the left (Tideswell Lane).
3. In 300 yards turn right at the 'Footpath' sign, and follow a narrow path between houses.
4. Cross three fields, keeping straight on.
5. Follow a path by a wall on your left, and cross a stile.
6. Keep straight on through six fields.
7. Cross a walled track to a stile opposite, then keep straight on and cross a ladder stile, signposted 'Foolow'.
8. Cross a field, bearing slightly left, to a stile signposted 'Foolow'.
9. Cross two fields, diagonally right, to stiles opposite.
10. Walk up a short incline to a stile, and follow a path with a wall on your left.
11. Follow the path through four fields, keeping straight on, and cross a walled track.
12. Cross the next field diagonally right to a stile.

13. Turn left on the road to Foolow.
14. At the village pond turn right on the road signposted 'Bretton'.
15. Continue along this road for one mile, bearing right at the top of the hill to *The Barrel Inn*.
16. Keep straight on past *The Barrel Inn* and in 100 yards go over a stile, signposted 'Public footpath to Eyam'.
17. Turn right, following the footpath downhill, cross a stile, and follow a path diagonally left.
18. Cross a stile, keep straight on for 50 yards, and then bear right down a field to a stile by a gate.
19. Turn left along a track, and on reaching the fluorspar works, bear right between the sheds.
20. Pass a pond on your right and keep straight on.
21. At the main road turn left, keep straight on for ¾ mile to Eyam, and turn left to the car park.

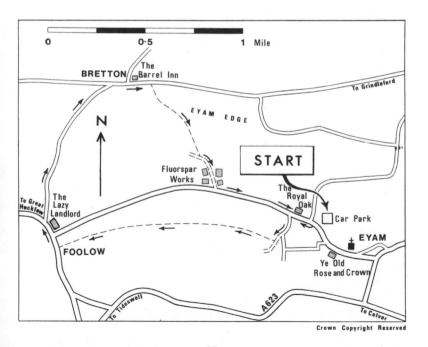

Crown Copyright Reserved

Great Hucklow – Grindlow – Foolow – Great Hucklow

STARTING POINT: *The Queen Anne*, Great Hucklow

PARKING: In Great Hucklow.
              No official car park.

WALK DESCRIPTION: If you are not feeling particularly energetic, but would like a relaxing stroll along quiet rural lanes and through level meadows, then you will enjoy this short, easy walk. Leaving Great Hucklow, you first pass through the quiet hamlet of Grindlow, and continue through meadows to Foolow. A short stretch of road walking follows, and you then join a track which leads past Brosterfield Farm to the fields beyond. Continuing along tracks through a shallow valley, you return to Great Hucklow by country lanes.

ROUTE INSTRUCTIONS:

1. With *The Queen Anne* inn on your right, walk along the main street, and take the second road on your right, signposted 'Grindlow'.
2. Pass through the hamlet of Grindlow, and where the road turns right, follow a path on your left signposted 'Public footpath'.
3. Follow a walled track for ¼ mile, and pass through a stile.
4. Keep straight on, crossing three stiles.
5. Turn left along a road into Foolow.
6. Continue on the main road through the village, and turn right opposite *The Lazy Landlord* inn at the signpost 'Wardlow'.
7. In ¼ mile turn right at the signpost 'Wardlow', and immediately turn right at Brosterfield Farm, signposted 'Public footpath to Stanley House'.
8. Keep on a track to the left of the farm, and at a second house, keep left and then right, following a wall.
9. Cross a stile and keep straight on, with a wall on your right.
10. Where the wall ends, veer slightly right across a field, and cross a stile.
11. Keeping straight on, cross three more stiles, and at a farmhouse, cross a stile and turn right along a walled track.
12. In 350 yards, turn left along a walled track, and follow the track to the road.

13. Cross the road and follow a minor road opposite, signposted 'Grindlow'.
14. Walk through Grindlow, and at the T junction, turn left into Great Hucklow.

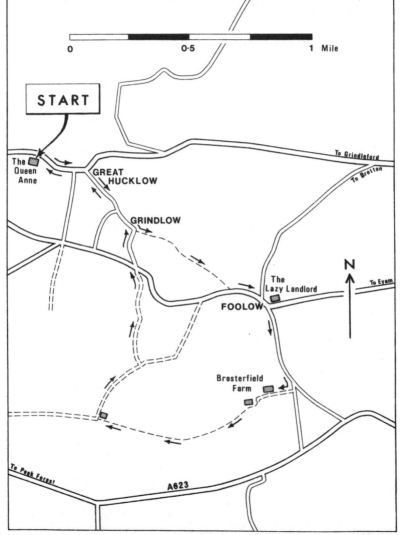

Great Longstone — Rowland — Great Longstone

STARTING POINT: *The White Lion,* Great Longstone.

PARKING: In Great Longstone.
No official car park.

WALK DESCRIPTION: The small village of Great Longstone consists mainly of one street, with the village green and cross at one end. You leave Great Longstone, passing the 13th century church, and follow field paths through meadows to the tiny hamlet of Rowland. You then cross the Great Longstone to Hassop Road, and follow a path which goes alongside the boundary of Hassop Park. This path leads you to the main road and onto the Monsal Trail, a disused railway which is now used as a track for walkers and cyclists. A pleasant walk across meadows takes you back to Great Longstone.

ROUTE INSTRUCTIONS:

1. Take the road opposite *The White Lion* in Great Longstone, signposted 'Rowland/Hassop'.
2. After the right-hand bend, and just beyond a bungalow, turn left along a walled track for 50 yards, and then turn right along another walled track.
3. Leave the track where it bends left, and keep straight on through a stile.
4. Cross a small field and a long narrow field.
5. Cross a track through two stiles, and then keep straight on to the stile 50 yards along the opposite wall.
6. Cross a field to a stile by a gate, and keep straight on to a stile immediately opposite.
7. Keep straight on to a stile, cross a field, and then go through two adjacent stiles.
8. Keep straight on, passing through two more stiles, to Rowland, where you turn right along the lane.
9. On reaching the T junction, cross the road, bearing slightly left, and take the track signposted 'Bakewell'.
10. Go over the stile on the right, beside a gate, and turn left along a path, with a high stone wall on your left.
11. Cross three stiles, and then bear right across the field, in the direction of a gate to the right of a house.

12. Cross a stile, turn left on road for 80 yards, and turn right through a gate opposite Toll Bar House.

13. Go through a swing gate and turn right onto the Monsal Trail.

14. Cross a road bridge, go under a bridge, cross another road bridge, and in 100 yards turn right off the Trail and descend steps.

15. At the bottom of the steps cross a stile and keep straight on.

16. Go through a stile and keep straight on towards houses.

17. Go through two more stiles onto a track by a house.

18. Turn left on the track and right along a road.

19. At the T junction turn right.

20. At the main road turn left to Great Longstone.

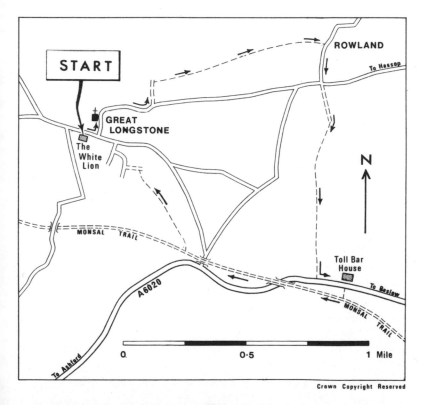

Crown Copyright Reserved

Grindleford Station – Padley Gorge –
Longshaw Estate – Grindleford Station

STARTING POINT: Grindleford Station approach road.

PARKING: Grindleford Station approach road.
Directions: From Grindleford bridge, take the B6521 Sheffield road, and in ½ mile, just past *The Maynard Arms Hotel,* bear left down a lane, and park on the lane, near a cafe.

WALK DESCRIPTION: From the Grindleford Station approach road, you cross the railway bridge over the entrance to Totley tunnel and follow a track through Padley Mill. From here you climb a track which leads to the beautiful Padley Gorge. On leaving the gorge, the path continues on open moorland by the Burbage Brook. You eventually enter Longshaw Estate, which is National Trust property, and pass Longshaw House. This was formerly the Duke of Rutland's shooting box, but it is now converted into flats. The return to Grindleford station is by pleasant paths through the estate.

ROUTE INSTRUCTIONS:

1. From the Grindleford station approach road, cross the railway bridge and follow a track which bears left to Padley Mill.
2. 40 yards past the mill, turn right on a track which leads up a hill.
3. Enter Padley Gorge through a swing gate, and follow a rocky path through the woods, keeping to the main track, with Burbage Brook on your right.
4. On leaving the wood, cross the second bridge, turn left, and in 30 yards bear right up the bank.
5. In 30 yards bear right to join a wider path.
6. Keep straight on and go through a small wicket gate onto the main road.
7. Cross the road diagonally right and enter the Longshaw Estate.
8. Follow the drive to Longshaw House and turn right down steps marked 'Footpath'.
9. Pass through two opposite wicket gates onto a wide grass track.
10. Follow the track for ¾ mile.
11. Pass through a gate and in 300 yards turn right over a ladder stile.

12. Descend to the bottom of a field, bear slightly left, cross a stream, and ascend a steep path at the extreme left of a wood.

13. In a few yards turn right over a ladder stile.

14. Follow a track through the wood and, on reaching houses, turn right down a lane.

15. On reaching the main road, turn right for 30 yards and bear left down a track to the Grindleford station approach road.

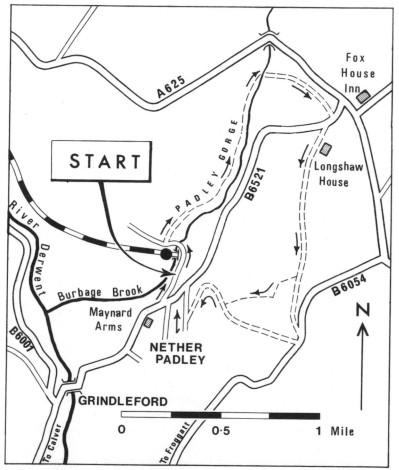

Hartington – Beresford Dale – Wolfscote Dale – Biggin Dale – Hartington

STARTING POINT: *The Devonshire Arms*, Hartington.

PARKING: In Hartington. Numerous places in the centre of village.

WALK DESCRIPTION: Following footpaths beside the river Dove, this walk passes through lovely Beresford, Wolfscote and Biggin Dales. Leaving the spacious village centre of Hartington, with its attractive duck pond, a path leads through fields and woodlands to Beresford Dale. In the dale is Pike Pool, with its pinnacle of limestone rock rising from the water. Continuing along the wooded cleft of the dale, you cross the river to enter Wolfscote Dale, with its smooth, grassy slopes rising steeply on either side. At the end of the dale, where high pinnacles of rock rise on each side, you turn into Biggin Dale, where wild flowers grow in profusion in the summer months. Following this valley around Wolfscote Hill, you return by bridlepaths and lanes, passing Hartington Hall Youth Hostel, to your starting point at Hartington.

ROUTE INSTRUCTIONS:

1. With *The Devonshire Arms* on your left, walk along the road signposted 'Warslow', and in 100 yards turn left by the toilets, at the signpost 'Public footpath to Dovedale'.
2. Follow the well-trodden path, with a wall on your right, and cross a walled track over two stiles.
3. Cross two fields and stiles, keeping in the same direction.
4. Follow the path uphill by wall, keeping by wall when it bends right.
5. Pass through a stile and enter a wood, following the path to the river.
6. Cross the bridge to the other side and follow the riverside path.
7. Cross another bridge and turn right at the signpost 'Public footpath to Wolfscote Dale'.
8. Go through two stiles at entrance to Wolfscote Dale and straight on.
9. Continue along the smooth-sided dale until you pass between pinnacles of rock on either side of the path, and at the end of this section, just before reaching a stile, turn left along Biggin Dale.
10. Keep to path at the foot of dale, passing through two stiles beside gates.
11. Where the dale forks, turn left over a stile at the signpost 'Hartington, Public Bridleway', and follow the footpath at the foot of the dale.

12. In 200 yards turn left at the signpost 'Public Bridleroad to Hartington', and climb the hillside to a stile by a gate.
13. Continue along walled path, and at crossroads of tracks, keep straight on.
14. Continue along the surfaced lane for ¾ mile, and when the lane descends steeply, turn left, and left again into Hartington.

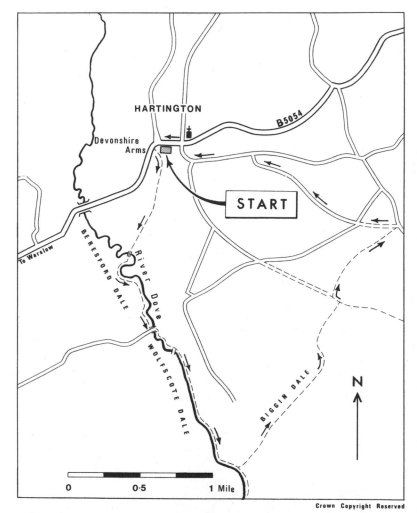

Crown Copyright Reserved

Hathersage – Shatton – Offerton Moor – Leadmill Bridge – Hathersage

STARTING POINT: *The George Hotel*, Hathersage.

PARKING: Hathersage Car Park.
Directions: Take the B6001 Grindleford road, opposite *The George Hotel*, for 300 yards. Turn left, and the car park is on your left. From here walk back to *The George Hotel*, in the centre of Hathersage, to start your walk.

WALK DESCRIPTION: On this pleasant riverside walk, which involves only a short climb, you leave Hathersage by quiet lanes, through a residential area, cross the main road, and go through fields to the banks of the River Derwent. Crossing the river by large stepping stones, at a beautiful spot on the river, you follow a riverside path to the quiet hamlet of Shatton. From Shatton there is a climb up a steep lane to the moors, where you will be rewarded with an extensive view of the Hope Valley. A moorland path descends to Offerton Hall Farm, and from there you descend by field tracks, to a riverside path. A pleasant walk along the river brings you to Leadmill Bridge, on the Hathersage-to-Grindleford road, and an easy walk through meadows and along tracks leads you back to Hathersage.

ROUTE INSTRUCTIONS:
1. With *The George Hotel* on your right, walk along the main road for 50 yards, and bear right up Jaggers Lane.
2. Keep on until you reach a cottage on the left with a millstone.
3. Bear left across a field.
4. Bear diagonally right, and cross the railway by two ladder stiles.
5. Cross the main road to the stile opposite, signed 'Public footpath'.
6. Bear diagonally right across the field, and follow path beside the Derwent.
7. You will eventually see large stepping stones across the river – cross these, and turn right at signpost 'Public footpath to Shatton 1½ miles'.
8. Follow the riverside path until you pass through a stile onto a lane.
9. Turn left up the lane to the village of Shatton, keeping straight on.
10. On reaching a junction of roads, one of which has a sign indicating a ford, bear left up the hill, and follow a lane with a stream on the right.
11. Climb this lane for ¼ mile, bend left, and continue for another ¼ mile.
12. Where the track bends right (just after two P.O. stones) turn left over a ladder stile signed 'Public footpath'.

13. The track is at first level, then gradually descends the hillside and continues alongside a wall.

14. On nearing a farm (Offerton Hall), pass through a stile and turn left down the lane towards the farm.

15. The lane bends left through an iron gate, passes the farm on your left, and then turns right, signed 'Unfit for motors'.

16. Go through first gate on your right, and bear diagonally left down field.

17. Cross a stile and descend the field.

18. Cross another stile, still descending.

19. Turn right at signpost 'Public footpath to Leadmill', and follow the path, with the river on your left, for 1½ miles.

20. On reaching the main road, turn left across Leadmill Bridge, and then immediately left through a stile.

21. Pass on the right of a copse of trees, and cross a stile.

22. Cross a stile by a house, and turn left along a lane.

23. Pass under the railway bridge and continue along the lane to Hathersage, turning left to *The George Hotel* or right to the car park.

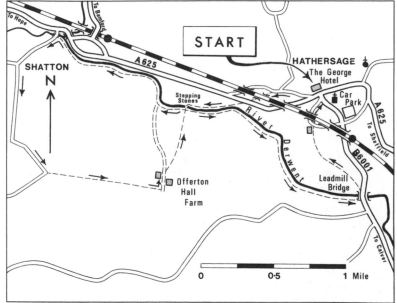

Hathersage – Brookfield Manor –
Birley Farm – Hathersage

STARTING POINT: *The George Hotel,* Hathersage

PARKING: Hathersage Car Park.
Directions: Take the B6001, Grindleford road, opposite *The George Hotel,* for 300 yards. Turn left and the car park is on your left. From the car park, walk back to *The George Hotel,* in the centre of Hathersage, to start your walk.

WALK DESCRIPTION: This is a short leisurely stroll from the village of Hathersage along a very peaceful valley to Brookfield Manor. From the quiet lanes ascending from Brookfield Manor, you will see in the distance, Hathersage and the church, picturesquely situated in lovely countryside. Descending to the valley again, you follow field paths to the fourteenth-century Hathersage church and go past what is reputed to be the grave of Little John, the friend of Robin Hood. From the church an interesting walk through the old part of Hathersage leads you back to the centre of the village.

ROUTE INSTRUCTIONS:

1. With *The George Hotel* on your left, walk along the main road, and in 300 yards, turn left along the lane beside *The Hathersage Inn,* signed 'To the Church'.

2. Continue along this lane, passing a cricket ground on the left and three houses on the right.

3. Cross three stiles, and then in 200 yards bear left at the signpost 'Footpath' towards a modern building.

4. Cross a stile and proceed along a fenced path.

5. Keep straight on and bear right alongside a fence to a wicket gate.

6. Turn left along the lane and keep straight on for ¾ mile.

7. Shortly after passing Birley Farm, turn left at the T junction (Cogger Lane).

8. Walk along this lane for ¼ mile, and on reaching houses, turn left over a stile beside the restriction sign.

9. Walk down the slope, with the fence on your right.

10. Go over a stile and continue straight on down the hillside, keeping on the left of a row of trees.

11. Go across a private drive and keep straight on to the stream.

12. Cross the bridge and follow the path to the right.
13. Pass through a stile, and immediately bear left up path towards church.
14. Turn right along the track for 50 yards.
15. Go over a stile on your left and walk diagonally left up the field towards the top end of a long stone wall.
16. Go through a wicket gate into the cemetery.
17. Opposite church door, bear right on narrow path to 'Little John's grave'.
18. Turn right down stone steps between two houses, and follow a stone path.
19. Turn right down the lane and turn right at the road.
20. On reaching the A625, turn right into Hathersage.

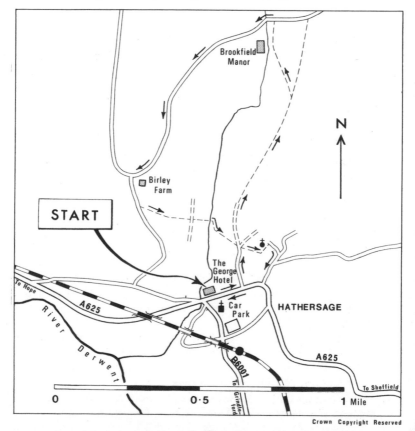

Surprise View Car Park — Millstone Edge — Higger Tor — Carl Wark — Burbage Brook Surprise View Car Park

STARTING POINT: Surprise View Car Park.

PARKING: Surprise View Car Park:
Directions: From Hathersage, take the A625 Sheffield road, and in 2 miles, just after passing through a rocky cleft, turn left into the car park.

WALK DESCRIPTION: This moorland walk, with superb views over Hathersage and the Derwent Valley from Millstone Edge, takes you beneath the high rocky ridge of Higger Tor and then across the moors to Carl Wark, a fortified hill. You may, if you wish, walk around the base to the right to see the ancient fortifications and climb to the top for extensive moorland views. The walk continues to a delightful picnic spot in the valley, and continues beside Burbage Brook on a moorland path.

ROUTE INSTRUCTIONS:

1. At the western (Surprise View) end of the Surprise Car Park, there are two stiles. Cross the one at the far end, and follow a narrow path which veers very slightly right across moor, keeping almost parallel to road.
2. On reaching fence along Millstone Edge, turn right, with fence on left.
3. Keep straight on, with the fence on your left all the way, and when the path descends steeply, turn left at the fence corner.
4. In 40 yards, turn right along a path which crosses the moor below two rocky outcrops.
5. Where the path reaches a wall, keep straight on.
6. Do not bear left with the main path where it descends to the road, but keep straight on a minor path, walking in the direction of the high rocks of Higger Tor.
7. When this path bends to the left, keep straight on, cutting across the moor for 100 yards (no path), and turn right along a narrow path which runs parallel with Higger Tor rocks.
8. When you reach a wide track, turn right.
9. On approaching Carl Wark, do not ascend to the top, but bear left around the base. (For viewing Carl Wark, see Walk Description).

10. Descend a path to the bottom of the valley to the right-hand tip of a fir wood, and go across a bridge and another stream.

11. Turn right and follow a path with the stream on your right.

12. Join a wide track, pass through two gateposts, and in 50 yards turn right along a path to a stile.

13. Cross the main road and go through a wicket gate at the signpost 'Footpath to Padley'.

14. Follow the path, keeping right, cross a bridge and immediately turn left.

15. On reaching a bridge, turn right along a path to a swing gate.

16. Cross the main road to a stile opposite, and turn left along a path near a fence.

17. Keep on the path by the fence back to the car park.

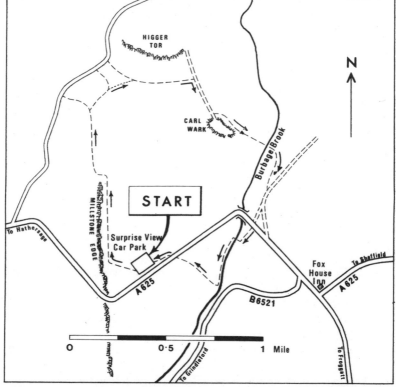

Hope — Hope Brink — Wooler Knoll — Hope

STARTING POINT: *The Old Hall Inn,* Hope.

PARKING: Car Park adjacent to *The Woodroffe Arms,* Hope.

WALK DESCRIPTION: Hope, with its 14th century church, is a popular centre from which to explore the Hope Valley and its surrounding hills. This walk leads you onto the slopes of Win Hill and back to Hope along moorland paths. Starting with pleasant, level walking by the riverside and along lanes, you soon begin to climb the slopes of Win Hill to Hope Brink. Here walking becomes easier, and the moorland track along Hope Brink to Wooler Knoll gives you good views of Lose Hill and the Vale of Edale. Shortly, at the turning point of your walk, a track leads down the hillside to a lane which passes Fullwood Stile Farm, and a level walk along lanes returns you back to Hope.

ROUTE INSTRUCTIONS:

1. With *The Old Hall Inn* on your left, walk along the main road for ¼ mile to the river bridge.
2. At the far end of the bridge turn left over a stile.
3. Follow a path beside the river, crossing two stiles.
4. On reaching a large house, keep left over a stile and follow a drive which goes to the left of the house.
5. At the lane, turn right.
6. Pass under a railway bridge, and immediately turn right on the track marked 'Public footpath'.
7. At the top of the fenced track, keep straight on through a wicket gate and continue up the hill.
8. Pass through a farmyard and keep straight on up a steep field.
9. At the field boundary wall, turn left, with the wall on your right, at a signpost 'Wooler Knoll'.
10. Continue along this path for about ¾ mile, and when it joins a main path, bear left.
11. In ¼ mile, at a junction of paths, bear left, away from the pine woods.

12. Just before reaching a gate and a stile, turn very sharp left along a track.

13. This track eventually leads downhill into a minor road and crosses the railway.

14. On reaching the main road, turn left and keep straight on to Hope.

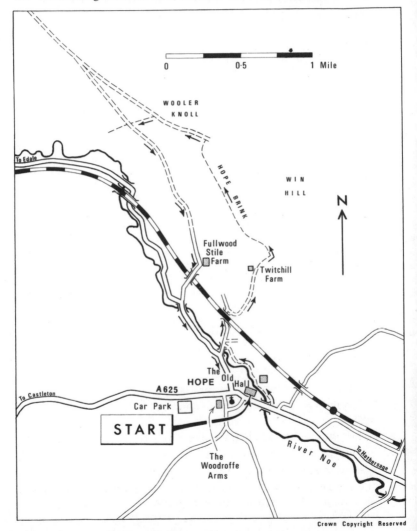

Dovedale Car Park – Ilam – Ilam Hall –
Paradise Walk – Ilam – Dovedale Car Park

STARTING POINT: Dovedale Car Park.

PARKING: Dovedale Car Park.
Directions from Ilam: Leaving Ilam on the Thorpe road, turn left
in ¾ mile, at the signpost 'Dovedale Car Park'.
Directions from Thorpe: Take the Ilam road and turn right in ¾
mile at the signpost 'Dovedale Car Park'.

WALK DESCRIPTION: Nature-lovers will find this walk full of interest,
since part of the walk is along a nature trail, in an area owned by the National
Trust. A Nature Trail leaflet can be obtained from the National Trust Office at
Ilam Hall, which gives information on rare trees, plants, flowers and birds to
be seen along what is known as Paradise Walk. Your walk commences at
Dovedale Car Park, from which point walks can be made into Dovedale. You
cross fields to the village of Ilam, and walk along the drive with its magnificent
trees to Ilam Hall (now a Youth Hostel). Passing in front of the hall you reach a
path which runs alongside the River Manifold. As the path veers away from
the river, you continue along what used to be a terrace in the gardens of the
Hall, and pass the Battle Stone, which commemorates a battle between Saxons
and Danes. Leaving the riverside path, and climbing a slope to the top of a
bank, you have a good view of Ilam Hall and grounds. The walk passes
through Ilam Hall courtyard, and returns to Ilam past the Church of the Holy
Cross. You return to the car park on the same path used at the commencement
of the walk. For a short stroll you can park in Ilam Hall car park.

ROUTE INSTRUCTIONS:

1. Cross the stile opposite the car park entrance.
2. Follow the sign 'Public footpath to Ilam', and in 50 yards bear right to a
   stile.
3. Follow the footpath, heading towards a wooded valley in the distance.
4. Go through a stile onto a track, and in 150 yards bear left to the road.
5. Turn right along the road to Ilam monument.
6. At the monument, turn right along the road signposted 'Alstonefield and
   Wetton', for 100 yards, and then bear left and go through the entrance to
   Ilam Hall.

7. On reaching Ilam Hall, turn left, and go down steps, turning right on reaching the riverside path.

8. Where the path diverts from the river, go along a terrace, passing the Battle Stone.

9. Cross a stile by a gate, and immediately turn sharp right, following a track up the hillside.

10. In 150 yards bear left to the crest of the hill, and walk diagonally right in the direction of Ilam Hall.

11. Go through an iron gate to the Hall courtyard.

12. Pass under an archway, and in 50 yards bear right onto a path which passes to the left of the church.

13. Pass through two wicket gates, and turn left on the track leading to Ilam village.

14. Turn left at the monument, and left again onto the path leading back to the car park.

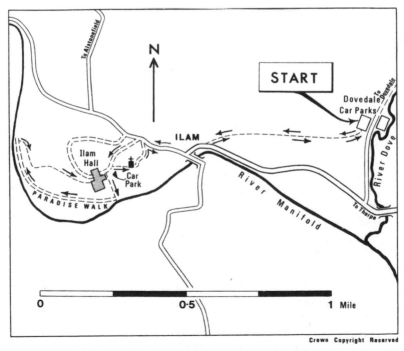

Dovedale Car Park — Ilam — Coldwall Bridge — Thorpe — Lin Dale — Dovedale Car Park

STARTING POINT: Dovedale Car Park.

PARKING: Dovedale Car Park.
Directions from Ilam: Leaving Ilam on the Thorpe road, turn left in ¾ mile, at the signpost 'Dovedale Car Park'.
Directions from Thorpe: Take the Ilam road and turn right in ¾ mile at the signpost 'Dovedale Car Park'.

WALK DESCRIPTION: On this easy walk you first visit the picturesque village of Ilam, with its quaint and unusual tile-hung houses, and then follow a footpath beside the River Manifold to Coldwall Bridge. After crossing the bridge a long ascent leads you to Thorpe, and from there you descend Lin Dale, with the conical hill of Thorpe Cloud on your left. At the foot of the dale you cross the famous stepping stones over the River Dove, at the entrance to Dove Dale, and return to the car park along a very popular riverside walk.

ROUTE INSTRUCTIONS:

1. Cross the stile opposite the car park entrance.
2. Follow the sign 'Public footpath to Ilam', and in 50 yards bear right to a stile.
3. Follow the footpath, heading towards a wooded valley in the distance.
4. Go through a stile onto a track, and in 150 yards bear left to the road.
5. Turn right along the road to Ilam monument.
6. At the monument, turn left, cross the bridge, and then turn immediately left down steps to the riverside path.
7. Keep to the riverside path, go over a wooden stile, and walk through a wood.
8. Enter a large field, and after passing a bed of rushes, bear right and follow a narrow footpath.
9. At the broken wall, bear left to a gate, and keep straight on, keeping to the right of a clump of bushes.
10. Turn left and cross the bridge.

11. Keep straight on the wide track into the village of Thorpe.
12. Pass a church on your right, and then bear left.
13. Follow the road round to the right, and on reaching the main road, go straight across, and follow a path signed 'Public footpath to Dovedale.'
14. Go round to the left of the quarry and descend to the valley bottom.
15. Descend the valley and cross the Dovedale stepping stones.
16. Turn left and follow the riverside path back to the car park.

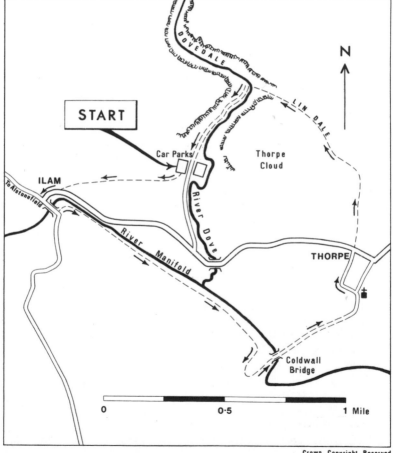

Litton – Litton Slack – Litton Mill –
Millers Dale – Cressbrook – Litton

STARTING POINT: The Village Cross, Litton

PARKING: In Litton.
No official car park.

WALK DESCRIPTION: From Litton, with its wide village street, village cross and stocks, you follow a quiet lane to the hamlet of Litton Slack. Soon you get a magnificent view of the beginning of Millers Dale and the hamlet of Litton Mill. The old railway can be seen on the opposite side of the valley. The Peak Rail Society has been formed for the purpose of restoring steam locomotives to operate this route and renovate stations and track. The track would run from Matlock, via Bakewell, to Buxton, and would cross the Monsal Dale and Millers Dale viaducts – a most scenic route. The walk leads into Millers Dale and passes through the yard of the Litton Mills nylon and textile mill. A magnificent walk along the River Wye and through a rocky gorge brings you to the open expanse of water known as Water-cum-Jolly. You then continue through the yard of the derelict Cressbrook Mill and make your way up the hill to the village of Cressbrook. From this road there is a panoramic view of Millers Dale. The walk continues along a quiet lane, with extensive views and a view on your right of Tansley Dale, just before reaching the village of Litton.

ROUTE INSTRUCTIONS:

1. With the village cross on your right, walk along the main road, signposted 'Tideswell/Millers Dale', and in 100 yards bear left up a lane marked with de-restriction signs.

2. In ½ mile, at a junction of roads, bear right on a road signposted 'Cressbrook/Monsal Dale', passing a cemetery on your left.

3. Just after passing a row of houses on your right, turn right along a lane signposted 'Litton Slack'.

4. Where the lane bends right to cottages at Litton Slack, keep straight on through a stile by an iron gate, and follow the grassy track, with a shallow valley on your right.

5. The track sweeps round in an S bend, passing an ancient chimney stack, and descends to the valley bottom.

6. The track leads to a lane which takes you into the hamlet of Litton Mill,

where you turn sharp left through gateposts marked 'Litton Mills'.

7. Walk through the mill yard and onto the riverside track, where, after passing through a rocky gorge, you enter a wide gorge known as Water-cum-Jolly.

8. Cross a bridge and pass through the yard of the old Cressbrook Mill.

9. On reaching the road, turn left and take the left fork, signed 'School', keeping straight on up the hill at the school.

10. Take the first turn right, and turn left at the T junction to Cressbrook village.

11. Pass the church and continue along the road, signposted 'Litton 1'.

12. On reaching the cemetery, keep straight on at signpost 'Litton ½'.

13. At Litton, turn left to your starting point.

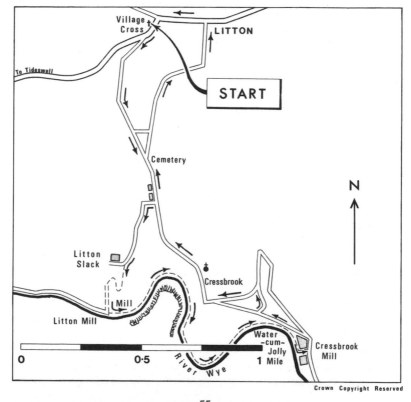

Monyash – One Ash Grange Farm – Lathkill Dale – Monyash

STARTING POINT: The Car Park, Monyash.

PARKING: The car park, Monyash
Directions from Bakewell: Approaching Monyash from Bakewell on the B5055, turn right at the crossroads in Monyash and there is a small car park immediately on your left.

WALK DESCRIPTION: The ancient village of Monyash is a former centre of leadmining. It has a 14th century market cross on the village green and a 17th century inn nearby. Leaving the village, the walk takes you along quiet tracks and field paths to One Ash Grange Farm. From the farm you descend a valley enclosed by craggy limestone rocks, and soon reach Lathkill Dale, a National Nature Reserve. Here you cross a bridge over the River Lathkill, then follow a footpath through the upper part of Lathkill Dale, and return to Monyash along a short stretch of main road.

ROUTE INSTRUCTIONS:

1. Turn right out of the car park, and keep straight on at the crossroads along Rake's Road.
2. In ¼ mile, just past the de-restriction sign, bear left along a track, and in 50 yards bear left at the signpost 'Public footpath to Lathkill Dale.'
3. Keep along the walled track at signpost 'Public footpath – Cales Dale 1½'.
4. At the end of the walled track, go over a stile, follow a path with a wall on your right, and then, in 50 yards, turn right over a stile. S.P. 'Cales Dale'.
5. Cross a field diagonally to a stile, and follow a path with a wall on your left at the signpost 'Public footpath to Youlgreave'.
6. Cross a stile, and follow a path with a wall on your left.
7. Before reaching the corner of the field, turn left over a stile and follow a path with a wall on your right.
8. Go through a gate and follow a wide track.
9. In One Ash Grange farmyard, just before reaching a row of cottages, turn left at the waymarked 'Footpath' sign on the corner of a barn, going round

the back of the cottages and bearing right towards the direction of the barns.

10. Pass through a stile by a barn and follow a footpath with a wall on your right, walking in the direction of a rocky valley.

11. Follow the path down the valley, passing beneath a limestone cliff, and ignoring paths on your right.

12. On reaching Lathkill Dale, cross the bridge and turn left along the valley bottom.

13. Continue through the dale for one mile, and at the main road turn left to Monyash.

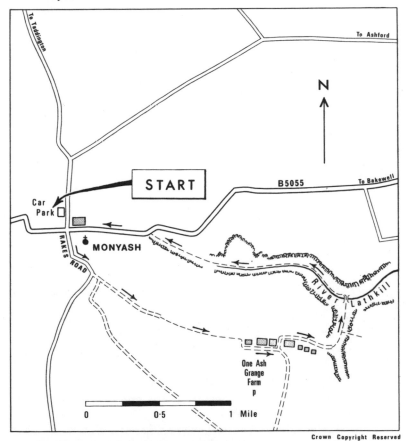

Crown Copyright Reserved

Over Haddon – Lathkill Dale – Conksbury Bridge – Raper Lodge – Over Haddon

STARTING POINT: Over Haddon Car Park.

PARKING: Over Haddon Car Park.
Directions from Bakewell: Take the B5055 Monyash road from Bakewell, and in one mile turn left at the signpost 'Over Haddon'. On reaching the village, turn right along the main village street to the large car park at the far end.

WALK DESCRIPTION: Descending steeply to Lathkill Dale by a rural lane from the car park, you will enjoy a quiet stroll through this lovely valley – one of the well-known Derbyshire beauty spots. At the end of this beautiful part of Lathkill Dale, you cross Conksbury Bridge and continue for a short while along a path beside the River Lathkill, through quiet meadows, before turning left, through woodland, up a steep path. The path continues through fields back to the road near Conksbury Bridge, where you follow a path through the fields above Lathkill Dale, with a magnificent vista over the dale. On reaching *The Lathkill Hotel*, you return to the car park along the main street of Over Haddon.

ROUTE INSTRUCTIONS:

1. From Over Haddon Car Park walk down the steep lane marked 'No Through Road'.
2. At the bottom of the hill turn left along the riverside path.
3. On reaching a road, turn right across Conksbury Bridge, and, in 200 yards, turn left through a stile.
4. Keep to the main riverside path, and on reaching a surfaced track, turn left, at the signpost 'Public Bridleway – Haddon Hall'.
5. Cross the river by a humped-back bridge and continue uphill on a narrow path through a wood.
6. The path leads on to a wide track.
7. At the top of the hill keep straight on and pass through an iron gate signposted 'Public Bridleway'.
8. Bear slightly right to a stile, and cross a field to the road.

9. Cross the road through two stiles.

10. Keep straight on across a field and go through a stile.

11. Go over a fence stile on your right and walk diagonally left to a wall stile.

12. Walk towards a stile to the right of *The Lathkill Hotel*.

13. Pass in front of the hotel, immediately bearing right, and then turn left along the main street through the village to the car park.

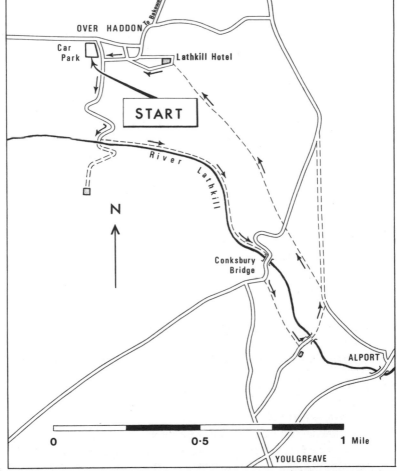

Crown Copyright Reserved

Tissington — Crake Low — Tissington Trail — Tissington

STARTING POINT: Tissington Trail Car Park.

PARKING: Tissington Trail Car Park.
Directions from Ashbourne: Take the A515 Buxton road, and in
3½ miles turn right at the signpost 'Tissington'. Keep straight on
to the far end of the the village and turn right into the car park.

WALK DESCRIPTION: This walk gives you the opportunity to visit one of
the most attractive villages in the Peak Park. You approach Tissington from
the main Buxton-to-Ashbourne road, passing along a fine avenue of lime trees,
and entering the large and convenient car park at the far end of the village.
Tissington is famous for its numerous wells, which, during the Well Dressing
Festival, commencing with Ascension Day, are decorated with large mosaic
pictures composed of flower petals, leaves and seeds, and having, usually, a
religious theme. The walk takes you past the village pond and along the much-
photographed wide village street, with Tissington Hall on the left and the
attractive Hall Well opposite. You go along lanes and tracks to join the
Tissington Trail, a disused railway, which is now used as a track for walkers
and cyclists. After walking for a short distance along the Trail, with good views
in the Parwich direction, you cross an old railway bridge and return to
Tissington by field paths and lanes.

ROUTE INSTRUCTIONS:

1. From the Tissington Trail Car Park, walk to the entrance and turn left
   along the road.
2. Go past the village pond and take the next right along the wide village
   street.
3. At the top of the street keep straight on, and in 500 yards, where the road
   bends to the left, bear right along a walled track signposted 'Public
   footpath to Parwich'.
4. Pass through two large fields, and then enter a walled track.
5. Keep straight on beside the left-hand wall to another walled track.
6. Bear slightly right across a field to a stile by a gate.

7. Turn right along the Tissington Trail.
8. Pass under a bridge and, 100 yards further on, turn left up a small bank in a hairpin turn, at the waymark 'Tissington and Parwich'.
9. Go through a stile and turn left across the bridge at the waymark 'Tissington'.
10. Pass through a farmyard and keep straight on up the field track, passing through a stile in a wall at the top of the field.
11. Cross two fields, keeping in the same direction, passing through stiles in the opposite walls.
12. Descend a large field to a stile in a wall at the bottom of the field.
13. Cross two fields and then turn left along the road.
14. Bear right with the road and, at the bottom of the hill, cross the road to the car park.

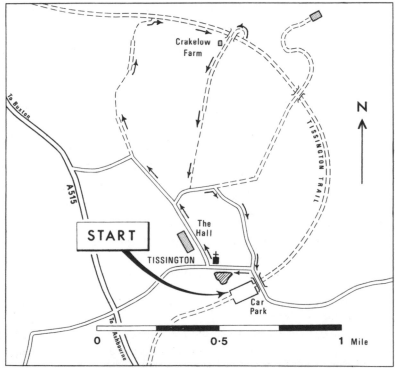

Wormhill – Cheedale – Blackwell –
Priestcliffe – Wormhill

STARTING POINT: Wormhill, on the main road, by the church approach road.

PARKING: In Wormhill.
No offocial car park.

WALK DESCRIPTION: On the path from Wormhill you enjoy a magnificent view over the tree-clad valley of Cheedale. Descending to a lovely spot beside the River Wye, you cross a bridge and climb the steep slopes on the opposite side of the river. As you approach the crest of the hill, pause to admire the view of Millers Dale on your left. When you reach the ridge, another view of Cheedale opens up on your right, with the now derelict track of the Buxton to Matlock railway running along the valley. The walk continues along lanes, passing through Blackwell Hall Farm, and descends to the road. A climb up the lane opposite takes you to Priestcliffe, and you then descend by a track to the main road. Here you enter the lower part of Cheedale, and return by a riverside path to the bridge you crossed at the beginning of your walk. A climb up the hillside leads you back to Wormhill.

ROUTE INSTRUCTIONS:

1. With the church a short distance away on your left, walk along the main road from the village, and 50 yards beyond the de-restriction sign, turn right at the signpost 'Public footpath to Cheedale and Blackwell'.

2. Follow the path, which swings left and descends to the river bridge.

3. Cross the bridge, and bearing slightly left, follow a waymarked path which swings right, and then continues steeply straight up the hillside.

4. At the brow of the hill, veer slightly left and pass through a waymarked gap in a wall.

5. Follow the path, with a wall on your left, and where the wall bends to the right, turn left over a stile.

6. Turn right along the edge of the field, and turn left, with the wall, at the corner.

7. At the end of the wall, by a waymarked post, turn right, go through a gate, and bear left along a track.

8. Go through a waymarked gate and keep straight on.

9. Continue along a walled lane, through a gate, and straight on through Blackwell Hall farm, bearing left onto a walled track.

10. Continue down the farm drive and turn left at the lane.

11. Cross the main road, and go up the road signposted 'Priestcliffe'.

12. When the road bends to the right, turn left along a track signed 'Unsuitable for motors'. At the main road, turn right.

13. Take the first turn left at the signpost 'Wormhill'.

14. In 30 yards, turn left and immediately left through a stile, onto the riverside path, following the Cheedale waymark.

15. Pass under a railway viaduct.

16. On reaching the river bridge, keep straight on, up the hillside, on the path used at the beginning of the walk. At the road, turn left to Wormhill.

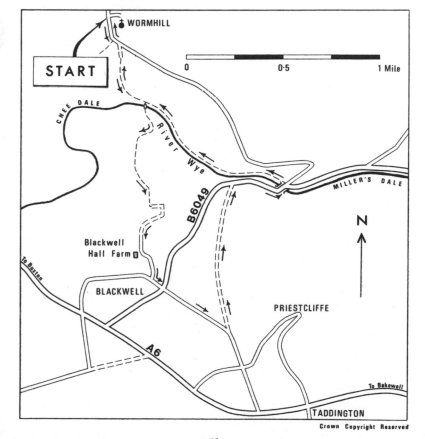

Wetton – Thor's Cave – Manifold Valley – Weag's Bridge – Wetton

STARTING POINT: Wetton Car Park

PARKING: Wetton Car Park.
Directions from Hartington: Take the B5054 Warslow road, and in 1½ miles turn left at the signpost 'Alstonefield/Wetton'. In 1½ miles turn right to Wetton. On entering Wetton, turn left, with *Ye Olde Royal Oak* on your right, and take the first turn right, on the Grindon road. The small car park is on your right.

WALK DESCRIPTION: For wonderful views of the Manifold Valley, this walk cannot be beaten, but do choose a dry day, as there are some steep slippery downhill paths to negotiate which are very muddy in wet weather. There are warnings along the route that the concessionary footpath leading to Thor's Cave (Point 4) must be taken at your own risk, but if you are sure-footed, and the walk is taken on a dry, calm day, there is no difficulty. After exploring the cave, which is set quite high on the slopes of a hill, you descend a long flight of steps to the River Manifold, which, at this point, runs underground in dry weather. You walk along the valley and cross Weag's Bridge before climbing steep lanes back to Wetton.

ROUTE INSTRUCTIONS:

1. From the car park, continue along the Grindon road, leading away from Wetton, and take the first turn right, signposted 'Wetton Mill'.

2. Turn left at signpost 'Wetton Mill/Manifold Valley', and in 25 yards turn left along a walled track waymarked 'Thor's Cave'.

3. Just after crossing a stile by a gate, turn right over a waymarked stile, and turn left down the field.

4. The path leads up and round to the right of the hill, passes over a stile, and descends quite steeply to Thor's Cave.

5. From the cave, descend the long flight of steps to the River Manifold.

6. Cross the bridge and turn left along the Manifold Valley.

7. Walk along the valley for ¾ mile, pass through a car park, and immediately turn left over Weag's Bridge.

8. Follow the road for ½ mile, and shortly after crossing a cattle grid, turn left towards the Wetton village sign.

9. Keep straight on to Wetton and the car park.

Thor's Cave ▶